Strength in Silhouette

Poems

Strength in Silhouette
Poems

T. L. Cooper

DEDICATION

The poems within these pages are dedicated to every woman, every person,
who has ever struggled to inhabit the strength within their hearts and minds.

ACKNOWLEDGMENTS

Loay Abu-Husein's photographic eye and skill with a camera not only brought my vision for the cover to life but enhanced it. I offer him my everlasting gratitude for all his hard work to make this cover what it is. Thank you not only for your work on the cover but your love and support over the years.

My eternal gratitude to Joanne Pence, Lori Felmey, Kelly Deaton, Trish Heath, Leslie J. Douda, Tony Haynes, Cynthia "Ariel" Evans, and Butch Knight for feedback on the cover!

My thanks to the members of the Facebook Groups, *Poet* and *Spiritual Poems*, for your feedback on individual poems included in this book as well as for your support and encouragement.

I offer my gratitude to all those who inspire and encourage me to keep writing!

I humbly offer the poems within to my readers with the hopes you'll find inspiration and encouragement to tap into your inner strength through my words. Thank you for your continued support!

The Love of My Life Redefined

The love of my life
Lives inside of me
She's never abandoned me
Even when I've denied her existence
She patiently waited for the end of my tears
So I could recognize and accept happiness
She held my hand
When I tried to bleed pain from my wrist
She held my head above water
When I thought I'd drown in despair
She sheltered my heart
When I willingly opened it to be shattered
She lifted my soul
When I fell over the cliff into regret
She breathed for me
When I allowed sorrow to smother me
She held on to rationality
When the wind scattered my thoughts
She loved me
Even when I hated me
She knew my strength
When I felt too weak to stand
She guided me toward the future
When I got stranded in the past
So today when I look in the mirror
I stare into the eyes of
The love of my life

Heart Chakra

My shoulders may not be wide
                    Never have been
But they are strong enough
                    Always have been
To hold your head when you cry
To offer you comfort when your heart breaks
To prop you up when you feel weak
To hold you high in celebration of your successes

My shoulders may not be wide
                    Never have been
But they are strong enough
                    Always have been
To hold my head high when I'm criticized
To square when my heart hurts
To meet my responsibilities
To lift me up in celebration of my accomplishments

My arms may not be muscular
                    Never have been
But they are strong enough
                    Always have been
To hug away your disappointments
To comfort your heartaches
To lend you strength when you feel weak
To raise in celebration of your success

My arms may not be muscular
                    Never have been
But they are strong enough
                    Always have been

To hug myself when no one else does
To comfort myself when my heart aches
To lend myself strength when I feel weak
To raise in celebration of my achievements

My hands may not have the tightest grip
                        Never have
But they are strong enough
                        Always have been
To hold yours when you need support
To give you assistance when you need help
To caress you when you need a gentle touch
To applaud your triumphs

My hands may not have the tightest grip
                        Never have
But they are strong enough
                        Always have been
To reach out for the connection I need
To accept comfort when offered
To caress my woes when I need gentleness
To applaud my victories

My lungs may not have the greatest capacity
                        Never have
But they are strong enough
                        Always have been
To offer you a breath when yours falters
To exhale a whisper of love to ease your pain
To hold a breath for you as you try something new
To release a celebratory cry for your happiness

My lungs may not have the greatest capacity
                        Never have

But they are strong enough
                              Always have been
To pull in oxygen when the act of breathing hurts
To exhale slowly the release of my pain
To hold my breath as I tell you my heart's desires
To release a celebratory cry for my own happiness

My heart may not be innocent
                    Never has been
But it is strong enough
                    Always has been
To understand your vulnerabilities
To offer compassion when you reach out
To reach out when you're unable to express your need
To love you without condition
To let you go if that's what's best for you

My heart may not be innocent
                    Never has been
But it is strong enough
                    Always has been
To allow myself to expose my vulnerabilities
To give myself compassion when I need it
To reach out when I need support
To love myself unconditionally
To let go of what isn't best for me

My shoulders, my arms, my hands, my lungs, my heart
All provide me the strength
To reach out
To love
To embrace life
To find my truth
Within my relationships

Within myself

Reaching out with
My shoulders, my arms, my hands, my lungs, my heart
I find strength comes back to me
Creating a circle of love, compassion, and strength
Allowing me to find my core and invite you in

Breathing Instructions

Breathing doesn't come with
An instruction manual
My teachers taught me
Breathing is autonomic
No learning necessary…
The body just knows how…
Inhale
Exhale
Inhale
Exhale
Yet there are times
When breathing fails me
When my body forgets how
When breathing requires
Instruction
I must instruct myself
Take a breath in
Let a breath out
Breathe deeply
Breathe evenly
Slowly fill my lungs
Slowly empty my lungs
Inhale
Exhale
Inhale
Exhale
Don't hold my breath
Don't forget to take a breath
Inhale
Exhale
Inhale

Exhale
Breathe in to a count of three or four or six
Breathe out to a count of six or eight or twelve
Until normal breathing returns
Until my body remembers to function
Until the chest crushing ends
Until the panic subsides
Inhale
Exhale
Inhale
Exhale
Eventually normal breathing returns
Allowing me to forget those
Moments when I need
An instruction manual
Just to breathe

Breath's Life

I shall breathe
Through it all
When life hurts
I inhale a cleansing breath
Allow it a moment to scrub away the pain
Then exhale fully
Letting all the pain flow out of my body

I shall breathe
Through it all
When life heals
I inhale an invigorating breath
Allow it a moment to energize my cells
Then exhale fully
Letting all the energy ignite me

I shall breathe
Through it all
When life disappoints
I inhale a satisfying breath
Allow it a moment to reassure my soul
Then exhale fully
Letting the reassurance guide me

I shall breathe
Through it all
When life exhilarates
I inhale a centering breath
Allow it a moment to calm my mind
Then exhale fully
Letting balance inspire me

I shall breathe
Through it all
When life takes my breath away
I inhale a living breath
Allow it to course through me
Then exhale fully
Letting breath revive me

I shall breathe
Through it all
When life changes directions midcourse
I inhale a settling breath
Allow it to propel me forward
Then exhale fully
Letting breath show me the right path

I shall breathe
Through it all
Until the moment I don't
When I finally inhale that final breath
I'll know I've lived the best I could
Allow it to course through me
Then exhale fully
Letting life leave me satisfied

Silk

White silk sheets cascade
Pile on top of me
Cover my body
Caress me
Shelter me
Flow through the air
Land one on top of the other
I lay still
Unable to move
Watching one layer of white
Pile on top of the previous
Cover my arms
Cover my legs
Cover my torso
Cover my face
I watch
Unable to stop them
Still the white silk sheets fall
Billow on top of me
Their white purity
Unreal, unnaturally bright
The silky texture slides over my skin
Luring me
Into a false sense of security
My breath strangles
My heartbeat quickens
I struggle to move
My arms
My legs
My torso
To push way

The rich silkiness
I see through the many layers
Your face blurred and confident
You pull the silk sheets away
For every sheet you remove
Four fall in its place
Your movements, your face
Become frantic
I sigh
There's no saving me
I appear blanketed in luxury
But you and I both know
The rich, silky texture
Steals my freedom
Cuts me off from the truth
Shelters me from reality
Lures me into ignoring the danger
I look up at your face as
The silky sheets slide right out of your hands
You're determined
To save me
From the choices I made
From the life I sank into
From the silk I once welcomed
I try to move the silk sheets away
It's up to me to save myself
I desperately attempt to free myself
Frozen in place
Eyes open so I finally see
Gasping for breath
Perhaps it's just too late
To escape
White silk sheets

Tied Up

You tied a white silk rope
Around my wrist
Around my ankle
Around my neck
I stroked it
I welcomed it
I cherished it
I called it a bracelet
I called it an anklet
I called it a necklace
I took it everywhere with me
It coupled me to you
I didn't see how the silky rope
Reigned me in
Kept me silent
Stopped my ascent
I never acknowledged the gentle but firm tug
You gave
Every time I stepped out on my own
Every time I spoke my mind
Every time I tried to soar
Until one day
The silk wore away
Exposing rough jute
Chafing my skin
But still I remembered the silk
And ignored the jute
Blood seeped out
Staining both silk and jute
As I felt my bonds grow ever restrictive
Until one day

I looked down and realized
You loosened your grip
You let the rope slip from your fingers
Because I no longer struggled
To step out on my own
To speak my mind
To ascend to my best self
I cried for a minute
Then picked up the rope
Untied the knots
Caressed the frayed edges
Kissed your fingers
And gently tied
The rope around
Your hands
Your ankles
Your neck
While you slept
You really should've held on tighter
Instead of letting that rope
Slip through your fingers
Because now I'm free

Work in Progress

My life
A work in progress
You asked me for perfection
I demanded my perfection
I thought I found the answer
To becoming a complete work
I became everything
I never wanted to be
Just to keep you
I forgot who I was
I left behind my truth
I squelched my strength
I extinguished my fire
I fixed everything you hated
I stopped my life
To give you your heart's desire
Only to have you throw
My lack of life back in my face
The love I desired from you
Smoldered as resentment in your eyes
Every attempt to edit
This work in progress
To meet your whims
Failed your scrutinization
One day I erased the whole
Work in progress
Stared at a blank page
The blank page of me
Backstory flooded the page
Reminding me
We can't escape yesterday

Our backstories create us
I remained a
Work in progress
Even when I lost me
Trying to fit your narrative
When I finally
Yanked back the pen
And wrote my own story
My inner strength developed muscles
My inner glow began to shine
My truth refused to be silenced
My imperfections began to breathe
My perfections found the light
I released the image you held of me
I rejected the story of me you'd written
I refused to accept that I was
Your work in progress
I embraced my own story
I became
Grateful to be
My own
Work in progress

Puzzle of Me

I looked for someone
To make me whole
After
I was smashed to the ground
Broken into pieces
Unrecognizable
Even to myself
I stared into a face I didn't know
I listened to a voice I couldn't remember as mine
I touched skin I could no longer feel though it covered me
I smelled a scent that no longer existed though it was mine
I cried tears that didn't fall
I screamed screams no one heard
I numbed myself to the world
I disappeared into bits
I looked at those smashed pieces lying on the ground
Pieces to a puzzle lacking familiarity
Without a guide to reassemble them, they made no sense
The edges no longer matched
The pieces of me lay there
Waiting, wanting, needing
Someone to put them back together
I begged for someone to reassemble the
Puzzle of me
I longed for someone to see me as whole
Rather than pieces of an unsolvable puzzle
Finally the day came
When I touched the pieces of
The puzzle of me
The first piece stung
So I dropped it

I tried another
The second piece sizzled
So I dropped it
I tried another
The third piece shriveled
So I dropped it
I cried real tears
Watched as the tears fell
On the pieces of me
Preserving them
Leaving them to wait for me
Because in the end
As much as I wanted someone else
To reassemble the
Puzzle of me
Only I could pick up the pieces of me
Only I could reassemble the pieces of me
Eventually the pieces of me morphed
The puzzle of me looked a bit different
Reassembly exposed my rough edges
Reassembly displayed my frayed pieces
Reassembly dulled the truth of me
Reassembly created a whole new me
One the old me found oddly familiar but better
The smashed pieces of me found form
A whole new image emerged
As I reassembled the
Puzzle of me

Reflection

The mirror reflects back
An image I don't quite recognize
It is me
Yet it morphs before my gaze
Hands force me to watch
Fingers chisel the change
When I look I see
Strength and femininity in battle
Innocence and knowledge in conflict
Yesterday and today melding
As I grow from girl to woman
The mirror reflects back
An image I don't quite recognize

Cast

You cast me in a role
I never wanted to play
Left me no choice
But to adopt the character
Pushed me live a life
I didn't recognize
Forced me to become someone
I didn't like
In that moment when you stole
My choice
You took away something deeper
Something I can never forgive
I lost all sense of me
In an act you casually dismissed
That I can never forget
You cast me in the role of victim
I wore it because I knew nothing else
Until one day I looked in the mirror
To see a survivor
From that day forward I vowed
To be a thriver
Victim erased my power
Surviving wasn't enough
Thriving, now that, felt powerful
While I wish I'd been strong enough
To not allow your actions to
Cast me in a role
I never wanted to play
The truth is
Your actions changed everything
They changed how I saw me

They changed how I interacted with others
They changed how I loved
They changed how I hated
They changed who I was
They trapped me inside a role
Never meant for me
A role you wrote and forgot
As you went about your life
Without a moment of regret
Today I recast that role
With one written especially for me
And embraced
The woman I was always meant to be

Masquerade

The masquerade ball where I live
Wakes me each morning
Shows me society's expectations
I paint on my smile
Give you what you want to see
Feel the pain in my heart
Of a million little criticisms
Of a gazillion little barbs
Of infinitely small moments
All surrounding the big event
That redefined me
Melted my core
Erased my surface
Evaporated my essence
Disintegrated my image of me
Forced me to create
A life in masquerade
Hiding the unacceptable me
Inside an acceptable shell
Tamping down what screams to break loose
I've come to realize that leaving
The masquerade ball where I've come to reside
Means not only exposing today's truth
But facing yesterday's suppressed reality
How can I expect others to not be ashamed
When I hide
That thing about me I want no one to know
The one I want to deny affected who I am
The one I hide with a false reality
The one I pretend doesn't mean anything
My not so secret secret

That forces itself through the cracks
In the beautiful masquerade of my life
Exposing my hypocrisy
As I both reveal and hide
Because I don't want to be defined
By that event that changed
Who I am forever
Because I don't want to give
Another that much power over who I am
 Forcing me to create
A masquerade ball of a life
Where I could pretend
It never happened
Where I hide even though
I know it wasn't my fault
Yet, somehow, I feel
Unworthy, guilty, damaged
Even as I know in my heart
I'm not the guilty one
I'm not the one who did wrong
I'm not damaged
I look in the mirror
See both
The masquerade of my life
And
The truth of my soul
The power of this woman demands release
The strength of this woman longs to cease concealment
The beauty of this woman breaks through the cracks
The imperfection of this woman screams for liberation
My masquerade ball has come to an end
Still, I cling to one last mask
The mask that protects me
From memory

From the betrayal
From the pain
From the reality
That can never be changed

Little Bit of Nothing

Little Bit of Nothing
That's what you called me
I protested vehemently the first time
In the end my protests were meek
Little Bit of Nothing
You assured me it wasn't an insult
Only a comment on my small stature
I chose to believe you
You were my friend
Yet every time you said it
Little Bit of Nothing
I felt diminished
I felt eclipsed
I felt weak
You shortened it to
Little Bit
With the reasoning
A nickname shouldn't be bigger than the person
Little Bit of Nothing
Not that Little Bit was better
Not really
Years later I realized
You always pulled that nickname out
Little Bit
Whenever I showed strength
Whenever I stood up for myself
Whenever I let you know I didn't need you
Whenever I shined too brightly
Whenever you couldn't contain me
I may have been small
Tiny even

But I was never a
Little Bit of Nothing
No matter how much you wanted me to be
No matter how much you pretended I was
No matter how many times you said I was
No matter what you believed
The nickname went dormant
When I shut you out
When I walked away
When I hid from you
After what you did to me
Yet I actually lost myself
Over the years
Until I felt like I was a
Little Bit of Nothing
I became exactly what I didn't want to be
I became exactly what I fought becoming
I became exactly what you pushed me to be
A woman who concealed her strength
A woman who capitulated to keep peace
A woman who needed too much to feel secure
A woman who didn't trust herself to make decisions
A woman who blew out her light before someone else could
A woman who acted like a
Little Bit of Nothing
No more
This Little Bit of Nothing
Refuses to be anyone's
Little Bit of Nothing
I will be
Every Bit of Me
A woman who revels in her own strength
A woman who is herself no matter the consequences
A woman who recognizes her needs but isn't needy

A woman confident she knows what's best for her
A woman who shines brightly in front of the whole world
A woman who bursts forth with happiness and love
A woman who loves herself
Too much to ever be cast as a
Little Bit of Nothing
I am me
I refuse to be less than the very best me I can be
I cannot, will not, ever be contained
I am so much more than a
Little Bit of Nothing

Refusal

You broke me
But I refuse to be broken
You shattered me
But I refuse to be shattered
You crushed me
But I refuse to be crushed
You smashed me
But I refuse to be smashed
See, in the end
I can bend, flex, morph
I can pick up the pieces
And glue me back together again
I may not be as beautiful or pure as I was
My cracks and repairs may show
My tender spots may bruise more easily
My calluses may refuse to soften
But the pieces all fit back together
Even if the edges are a little rougher
Even if the pieces chip more easily
Even if you see only the broken bits
Cobbled together by unsteady hands
In spite of your best efforts
To wreak havoc on me
I cannot, I will not, I must not
Be broken

Broken Doll

You saw
A broken doll
Cracked face
Split fingers
Scratched toes
Torn body
Knocked off a pedestal
Stored in an attic
Left behind, abandoned, forgotten
Rediscovered, dusted off, tossed in the trash
Broken, unsafe, unsavory
I saw
A beloved doll
Well worn with life
Tossed about, dragged around, lost
Played with, enjoyed, forgotten
Who didn't need fixed
Only loved for all the
Cracks in her surface
Tears in her depth
Treasured for her experience
Allowing the world to see
All she'd become
Rather than
The broken doll
You saw

Strength Given Away

I handed you my strength
Gave it to you willingly, without hesitation
You needed it more than I
You greedily soaked it up
Without so much as a thank you
I didn't mind
You needed it more than I
I comforted myself that someday
When I needed strength
You'd share some with me
Instead once you'd had your fill
When you'd drained me of all my strength
Left me weakened and vulnerable
You told me I no longer offered what you wanted
Never had really
I watched from the ground
While you towered over me
Holding the strength I happily handed you
Healed and ready to conquer life's offering
You told me not to be so dramatic
That you'd never taken anything from me
That I never gave you anything
That you did it all yourself
That I was only a burden
I watched your smug expression
You believed all you said
I closed my eyes and cried a tear of steel
Determined to release myself from your hold
You never deserved the strength I gave you
Even if you needed it more than I
As you sauntered away

Leaving me where I fell
I silently called to my strength
And felt it rise from within me
See, no matter how much I gave you
I held a tiny bit in reserve
Just enough to hold me together
When you stomped on my spirit
And I felt my heart splinter from the crushing weight
Of your incredible need to control me
You turned to look back
I stood in all my strength
Beautiful, strong, vibrant
Better without you
Drawing you back
You wanted more
But this time
I refused you my strength
Because you didn't deserve it
Even if you needed it more than I
So we battled
For control
Over the strength
I once readily handed over
You didn't expect that
But I'm too strong to capture
Because this time
I no longer believe
I no longer care if
You needed it more than I

Stray Dog

You captured me
Like a stray dog
Mangy, defensive, and a little wild
Tortured, tormented, and starving
You put me in a pretty little cage
Washed me
Fed me
Medicated me
Brushed me
Petted me
Patted my head
Took me on long walks
Told me I had potential
Decried those who abandoned me
Loved me
Offered me security
Gave me hope
Left me wagging my tail
At the sight of you
Mixed in with all that love
You never let me forget
You rescued me from my life
You gave me a home
When no one else wanted me
Every time I stood tall
You reminded me
You rescued me from
Life as a
Stray dog
Ensuring my obedience
Ensuring my loyalty

Ensuring my dependence
I hung my head, appreciative
In my heart I longed to
Escape my past
Escape the label
Be seen as more than
Your rescued
Stray dog

I Thought

I thought
Without you
I'd be nothing
What I failed to realize
Was
Your presence
Didn't increase my worth
Your desire
Didn't equal love
Your need
Didn't equal affection
Your attention
Didn't equal adoration
I thought
If you left
I'd die
I thought
Your strength
Somehow increased mine
So I hid behind you
Waiting for the day
When I'd be strong
Not knowing the wait
Weakened me daily
I thought
If I gave up
Everything that was me
I'd be a better person
I thought
If I molded myself
Into everything I hated

It had to be better than me
Then you would love me
Sometimes I wonder
Just why
I thought at all

Departure

I cannot leave me
You can
But I cannot
I have loved me
I have hated me
I have ignored me
I have pretended I didn't exist
I have believed I didn't matter
I have tried to leave me
But I cannot
When I loved me
You hated me
When I hated me
You loved me
When I ignored me
You showered me with attention
When I pretended I didn't exist
You reminded me I lived
When I believed I didn't matter
You convinced me I was important
When I tried to leave me
You anchored me in place
Yet in the end
When the day came
That I found enough strength
To truly love me
To stop hating me
To give myself attention
To revel in my existence
To accept that I was important
To want to be with me

You reminded me
I couldn't leave me
But you could
And you did
Somehow I found me
With your
Departure

Bared

Bared in front of you
Left to flail in my vulnerability
Naked to all who care to see, really see
Alone with all my emotions
My weakness sought your grasp
My strength weakened for your approval
My love abandoned me for your heart
My wisdom hid from your knowledge
All of me bare and yet concealed
All of me lost and yet found
All of me needed and yet rejected
All of me reached out for more and accepted less
Until one day
I stood
Left to embrace my vulnerability
Naked to myself if I cared to see, really see
Alone with all my emotions
Bared in front of me

Glass Courage

Glass-courage
Courage hiding behind a glass wall
Shatters as soon as the wall is breached
The prison wall you erected around me
Encapsulated me
Kept me quiet
Left me in tears
Broke me down
Gave me reason to adopt
Glass-courage to protect myself
When I lost my own courage
I stood inside the glass
Hiding in plain view
Courage fragile as blown glass
Ready to crack
At the slightest provocation
I ignored the hairline cracks that appeared
As I lived my life
Glass-courage
Breakable, fragile, unreliable
Protected me
Giving my real courage
A chance to heal
A chance to grow
A chance to shine
Real courage shattered
Glass-courage
Allowing me to survive
Allowing me to grow strong
Allowing me to thrive
Though I hope never need

Glass-courage again
I can finally feel grateful
For the role played by
Glass-courage

Dreamed of Being

Dreamed of being
Something other than I am
The image in my mind
A woman no one could contain
Head held high when life struck hard
Independent no matter the cost
Strength that couldn't be beaten down
Laughter sounding easily and often
A smile that beguiled and comforted
Standing tall without fear
Embracing risks that brought rewards
Calculating the move to bring success
Never relying on others for existence
Never needing a man
Refusing to just survive
Demanding only the best
Grasping whatever made her thrive
Always true to herself
Unconcerned with others opinion of her
Holding tight to her morals without judging others
Not letting anyone dictate her beliefs
Not allowing anyone to manage her emotions
Never allowing anyone to tell her what to think
That woman
The woman I was meant to be
Lost her way
Lost herself
Struggled to break free
Never accepted her role as inferior
Hid beneath what was expected
Screamed to be heard under the acceptable façade

Fights to breath
Is it too late to become
A woman impossible to contain
The woman I
Dreamed of being

Warrior Woman

I stand short but tall
Shoulders narrow but squared
Armor at the ready
Weapons stowed within reach
Trained for the moment
When you breach
My defenses
My smile slides into place
Fooling you into thinking
I'm easily taken
My gentle curves
And slight stature
Make me appear to be easy prey
To those who would seek to conquer
But when the battle you seek is done
You'll find yourself bloody and vulnerable
Your weaknesses exposed
Your losses incalculable
And you'll wonder how you missed
This tiny woman, as you saw me,
Held the strength of a
Battle hardened warrior

Chains

Voices echoed
Through the hurricane
A woman in chains
Searched for voices
To tell her erotica
Hoping the devastating winds
Wouldn't destroy her
Because she needed to
Live to tell
The pleasure of artful denial
The pain of secret desires
The beauty of the lightest kiss
The tingle of the tightest embrace
The thrill of the slightest touch along bare skin
The need for screams of pleasure
The ecstasy of dominating the dominator
The desire to break free from the chains
The world cast upon her
As she sought her most erotic desires
And struggled to escape the hurricane
Blowing through her life
In voices of criticism
As she sought to find
The balance between
The naughty and the nice
She discovered
Her power as she embraced both
The whore and the Madonna within
And broke the chains
Society insisted she wear

Hero to Villain

I've never been
Much of one for
Heroes
So when you showed up
Sword drawn
Ready to defend my honor
Ready to fix my life
Ready to erase all my past pain
I retreated into my fortress
Behind my smile
Where I felt safe as
I nodded but doubted
I expected you to
Turn the sword on me
As soon as you really knew me
I listened closely as you serenaded me
From the middle of the moat
Surrounding my fortress
Trying to find the deception in your promises
But hearing only sincerity in your voice
You promised to be my
Hero
Knight
Samurai
Warrior
When you promised to
Save me from myself
You went too far
I turned you into a villain
I may have been flawed
I may have made mistakes

I may have been hard to know
But
I never needed
Saved from myself
That was my job
Whatever my flaws
Whatever my weaknesses
Whatever my history
In the end
As much as I wanted
You to be my
Hero
Only I could save me
Only I had the power to release me
Only I had the power to be my
Heroine

Femme Fatale

Lights line the dark city streets
Secrets hide in the shadows
Those lonely souls exploring the night
Breathe in beauty and danger
Hidden in betrayal and double-dealing
Truths uncovered in the tight clothes
Of a femme fatale seducing
Criminal and detective
To hide her secrets and frame her man
The aphrodisiac of her mysterious aura
Filled with both need and independence
Keeping both
Under her spell
Reminding us all the
Mystery hidden in every woman
Is the strength and power
She both exudes and conceals
To play the odds in her favor
We would all be better served to
Embrace our inner
Femme fatale

Push Me Higher

Push me higher
High up into the sky
With a base to hold me
And a rope to cling to

Push me higher
High up into the sky
Where I feel like I'm flying
And all things are possible

Push me higher
High up into the sky
Past the tree tops
Until the sun shines on my face

Push me higher
High up into the sky
The wind on my face
My smile alight with pleasure

Push me higher
High up into the sky
Where I can see the whole world
And feel all the power within me

Push me higher
High up into the sky
Where you can no longer anchor me
And I'm free from your grasp

Push me higher

High up into the sky
Oh, forget it, I'll do it myself
You can never push me high enough

Winged Back

My self-destruction
Departs on your strong, winged back
Emptiness consumes me

My self-destruction
Chased you around the world but
You could not escape

I self-destructed
Flung my pain on your winged back
As you ran away

The Trade-off

I traded my self-respect
For your attention
I traded my confidence
For your approval
I traded my dreams
For your future
I traded my desires
For your needs
I traded my happiness
For your contentment
I traded my strength
For your support
I traded myself
For you
In the end
I lost not only me
But you
The trade-off
Hardly seems worth it
As I strive to
Regain my self-respect
I lose your attention
Regain my confidence
I lose your approval
Regain my dreams
I lose the future with you
Regain my desires
I lose your needs
Regain my happiness
I lose your contentment
Regain my strength

I lose your support
As I stand on my own
I wonder if I never sacrificed me
Would I still have lost you?

Wisps

Tiny wisps of me
Drift away
Into the night
Giving to the world
The essence of my soul
Showing you
The love in my heart
Dissolving me into
You
I struggle to maintain
A foothold
In the truth of me
Balancing my strength
Against your overwhelming desire
Securing my existence
Even as I watch
The darkness swallow
Tiny wisps of me

Released Bits

Little bits of me
Floated by unnoticed
Just as I wanted
If you saw you might try to fix me
I didn't want to be fixed
I didn't want to be saved
I didn't want to be reassembled
So I stood there
Watching me float on by
While you focused on
The nothing between the bits of me
I felt my bits find their way back
But they no longer fit in place
New growth replaced the dead bits
Leaving me morphed into
A stronger me
A better me
A new me
An unrecognizable me
When you saw how I'd changed
You tried to force the bits back on to me
The me you knew
Only to discover
There was no place to attach them
They no longer fit
They fell off and floated away again
I stood and smiled at you
Daring you to challenge me like you had before

Yin Yang

Without my darkness
I have no light
Without my light
I have no darkness
We come together
To form the perfect union
A union of life
Based on light and dark
Filling the gaps between
The beginning of me
And the end of you
Melding us together
In a form that creates
The circle that gives balance
To all within it
My brightness is only bright
In the face of darkness
My darkness is only dark
In the face of light
When you and I come together
We create a perfect union
Light and dark
Swirling, caressing, loving
One another
In a play of bare vulnerability
In a wave of revealed strength
In a union of shared truth
Every time we unite
We come together
To form the perfect union
Of shadow and form

Of perfection and imperfection
Of light and dark
Never forget you and I
We come together
To form the perfect union
A union of life

Intertwined

You handed me lace and ribbons
I grabbed your tie and hat
You gave me a frilly pink dress
I stole your dark suit
You curled my hair
I flattened it and tucked it under your hat
You told me to sit demurely with crossed ankles
I straddled your chair
You told me to be less forceful
I pushed you aside
You told me aggressiveness was unattractive
I demanded freedom
You encouraged me to be weak
I flexed my strength
You silenced my words
I screamed them for the whole world to hear
You wanted me to be ladylike
I gave you a wicked half grin
You said I was acting too masculine
My eyes twinkled
You told me no one loves women like me
I laughed until I cried and then laughed again
Because I know a secret
A woman's femininity
A woman's strength
Intertwined
Can never be contained

Two Faces

Two faces stare at me
From within my soul
One is quiet and demure
Sophisticated and acceptable
One is loud and brash
Wild and unforgiveable
One you love
The other terrifies you
One I love
The other saddens me
Unfortunately, like so much else,
We can't agree
Which face I should wear
I look in the mirror
My complexity stares back
Nice girl and naughty girl
Strong but imperfect
Respectable yet passionate
All things in one face
Appearing as two
In a woman who knows
She can never be
Anything less than
All she is
She can never accept
Anything less than
All she deserves
She can never give up
Her complexity
Nice girl and naughty girl
Two faces battling

From within my soul
Neither will ever win

Goddess

Power within
Emanates without
Drawing you in
Shining through you
Lifting you toward the sun
Smiling a crescent moon
Taking life to a higher heaven

Power within
Emanates without
Drawing you in
Darkening your being
Pushing you to the ground
Frowning a dark crevice
Smashing life into a lower hell

Power within
Emanates without
Drawing the world
Creating new life
Balancing dark and light
Celebrating yin and yang
Pushing life on Earth

Power within
Emanates without
Drawing us together
To find all our
Inner goddesses

Netted

Washed ashore
Tangled in your net
Drowned in your obsession
Bare, raw, revealed
Displayed for the casual observer
Left to disintegrate
Abandoned by your unmet expectations
Hardened by your possessiveness
Feigning weakness in my capture
Awaiting a drop in your guard
Relaxed in my knowledge you can't keep me netted
Released by my own strength

Cubic Zirconia

You're an idiot
I'm sorry to say that
No, I'm not
I opened myself to you
I laid myself bare in front of you
I offered you
A treasure worthy of royalty
But you never truly appreciated
The gem that I am
Someday you'll see that what you
Treated as costume jewelry
Was really a
Diamond awaiting the perfect setting
Strong, beautiful, and resilient
And ready to sparkle in the light
This diamond offered you love and pleasure
Instead you settled for cubic zirconia
Enamored by the convenience and price
The sparkle may seem the same
But cubic zirconia will
Never be a diamond

Feminine Feminist

Fearing not your attempted constraints
Embracing my gentle side
Melding into my strength
I never lose sight of life's beauty
Niceties offered to the world
In frilly dresses and power suits
Naughtiness expressed to all
Exalting my ability to overcome

Fighting to be seen for my actions
Equal as anyone to the task before me
Mired in the fight to control my life
Individual merits celebrated
Needing pleasure's touch
Indelible ink creating me
Standing beside, never behind
Treated with the respect I deserve

…I am a feminine feminist

Taking a Stand

I've kept my silence
Spoken no words
When I should've
Let my silence
Speak for me
When fear controlled me
And only I was at stake
But when I finally faced my fear
I exposed
Unfairness
Unethical behavior
Broken boundaries
To protect another
I put myself on the line
To say what no one else would
Suddenly I was the focus of suspicion
Did I speak the truth?
Was I just trying to cause trouble?
Could I prove what I stated?
As the questions came I wondered
Would others stand beside me?
Would others speak the truth?
Or would I find myself an outcast?
I stood up for others
And in the process discovered
I was worth standing up for

Tenderly

Hold myself tenderly
A concept foreign to me
I push myself into strength
I stand up tall
I project my power
I remind myself I can handle...
Anything, everything
Yet I rarely stop to
Hold myself tenderly
To give myself compassion
To give myself understanding
To treat myself how I would treat you
When I hurt
I tell myself
To get over it already
To just work through it
To let it go
But I rarely allow myself
The luxury of
Treating myself with tenderness
Holding myself tenderly
Allowing myself tears
Allowing myself to embrace my weaknesses
Allowing myself to feel the pain
Today I vow I will find
Strength in my tenderness

White Board

I am a white board
Filled with a flurry of ideas
Jamming thoughts into every empty space
Brainstorming possibilities
Revealing a plan
Telling all my secrets
Listing my desires
Concentrating on results
Erasing anything that doesn't work
Replacing the erased with new thoughts
Trying to find the right components
Bringing out the best of me
Leaving behind the worst of me
Trial and error
Smudges of failed attempts remain
Broken dreams mar the surface
Abandoned plans hide beneath new ideas
Lost moments beg for another chance
As I search for the right formula
As I combine concept after concept
As I try experiment after experiment
To create the perfect me
Striving to have the strength
To accept the perfect me
Will always be less than perfect
So I scribble away on the
White board of me
Searching for the impossible
But enjoying the process
That makes me become
A woman worthy of

Her place in the world

Blank Canvas

I am a blank canvas
Awaiting strokes of color
Bringing life to my existence
Taking me from bland to spicy
Uncovering my hidden brilliance
Realizing the beauty of acceptance
Creating the me I envision
Bold colors painted by experience
Teaching me strength and compassion
Undulating between sweet and tough
Revealing the multiple dimensions of me
Culminating in a woman I can love
Accenting the confidence drawn by passion
I am a piece of art in progress

Sketch

Trapped in your ink
Your pen drawing an image of me
I don't recognize
It's who you see
Perhaps it's who you want
Perhaps it allows you to love me
Perhaps it permits you to keep me
I pull away from the image you sketched of me
Looking down I saw it was merely
An outline the suited your needs
An image that left me flat and incomplete
I pull myself gently forward and up
Balance on my hands in cobra pose
Ready to strike an image all my own
Slowly I pull
My head, my shoulders, my stomach free
Remaining under your control
My hips, my legs, my feet
I panic
I need to be someone I recognize
I inhale deeply and relax
Wait for you to move your pen away
You're so intent on creating your image of me
You don't notice me pulling away, changing
Struggling will only prove you right
Make it appear I need contained
Give you license to protect me from me
Allow you to think I'm not ready to be whole
I wiggle to free your grip on your sketch of me
You draw another line to reaffirm your image of me
I slither a little deeper into myself

Freeing me from your sketch of me
Scarred by your creation of this image of me
I don't recognize
I breathe new life into myself
I become
Someone you don't recognize
I become whole
I'm who I see
I'm not perfect
But the perfect me
You are free to see who you want
Either your sketched image of me
Taking control
Becoming whole
Or
Me as a shattered image you fixed
Your image of me is beyond my control
All I can do is be
A woman worth knowing
A woman capable of giving and receiving love
A woman who is more than merely another's sketch
The woman I recognize

Embers of Strength

I found a tiny box
Tucked deep inside me
Its heat forced me to wear gloves
I held it gently
Sat on the ground - exposed, vulnerable
Feared the contents would burn me alive
Gently lifted the lid
Shining strength glowed
Sparked the embers within
Embers of strength floated out of the box
Warmed my cold atrophied spirit
Slowly teased me with possibility
Showed me hope
I watched the embers glow
Waiting for me to welcome its offering
Strength embraced me
The glow spread over my naked skin
I shivered in spite of its warmth
I closed my eyes and exhaled slowly
Allowing strength to encapsulate me
I realized I'd never lost strength
Only saved it until I was ready
To step into my truth
When I looked down
More strength glowed inside the box
An endless supply regenerating itself
Overflowing the box
The more I embraced strength
The more I knew the truth
The glow of inner strength
Emanates from each of us

When we find the courage to
Open the tiny box within

Inside This Glass

Sitting inside this glass
Surrounded, protected, trapped
Fearing the shards of glass
Cutting through me
Should I attempt to break free?
Should I risk
A million little cuts
Blood trickling around the shiny shards
Stinging pain spreading over my skin
Your hand so deftly holds the glass in place
Appearing gentle, almost ready to lift it
I curl into a ball
Put my head on my knees, hands on head
Try to hide my strength and my weakness
Waiting for a way to break free
My skin tingles fearing the damage
Courage builds inside me as I wait
I try to appear to have given up
Maybe you'll walk away
Allowing me to release myself from this glass
In my heart I know the only way to escape
Is to shatter the glass
Shards slicing into you and me alike
Every cut creating scars as reminders
Breaking free from any fortress - prison
Leaves everyone, even the captor, injured and altered

Pedestal

You
Placed me on a pedestal
Ornate and majestic
High above reality
You handed me a mask to wear
The me you wanted to see
I carefully placed the mask over me
Adjusted it
Adjusted me
But it was never me
It was only the image you saw
It was little more than a mirage
Of a woman who could never exist

You
Grew to dislike the mask
Asked what had become of me
Wondered where the woman you loved went
Denied the mask you'd handed me existed
Mocked the pedestal you'd placed me on
Turned your back and fled
As I sat on a pedestal
Above the reach of love

I
Removed the mask
Held it in my hand
Bowed my head
Cried tears I hid
Lost and alone
Trapped high on a pedestal

Unable to be
What you wanted
Lost to myself
Clinging to the mask
In hopes it would bring intimacy
Wishing I could drop the mask
Desiring to be truly seen
Waiting for the pedestal to crumble
Fearing the drop if I fell
Praying love's arms would catch me

Apology Queen

I am sorry, yet again
I mutter the words
I scream them
I proclaim them
I plead them
I am sorry
Over and over
Yet I'm not so sure I should be so sorry
I apologize at the slightest hint
I've offended
I've hurt
I've overstepped my bounds
I've disappointed
And yet
How often am I really sorry?
I wondered tonight
Because I often utter the words
I am sorry
As a preemptive strike
A kindness bomb
A humility missile
A disarming air strike
When did this happen?
When did I become "Miss Apology Queen"?
It's almost as if I somehow decided
To apologize for my very existence
And yet I remember a time
When an apology had to be
Coaxed from my lips
When I believed
An apology

Should be deserved
Should be a result of a real transgression
Should mean something more than
"Love me. I'm good. I promise."
Shouldn't be a way of saying
"I'm sorry I'm not perfect.
I'm sorry I'm not what you want.
I'm sorry I'm not weak enough for you.
I'm sorry I'm so... me"

Strength

When I stand tall
You push me down
When I embrace me
You try to squash me
When I speak my truth
You stifle my voice
When I refuse to be quieted
You find fault with my words
When I refuse to shrink
You criticize my core
When I refuse to fit your image of me
You cut me with your definition of me
When I exude confidence
You bruise me with my imperfection
When I refuse to be controlled
You chain me to my past
When I stand in my strength
You point out my weaknesses
When you try to corral me
I break the fences
Apparently I'm too much for you

Branded

You branded me
In bold letters, well, at least one
For all to see
Expressing the truth as you saw it
The bright red 'A'
Speaking volumes to all who approached
Assumptions made by all
But many words begin with 'A'
Yet, everyone knew what you meant
However, I wore your 'A' boldly, proudly
Though a bright red 'B'
Might have fit me better
Or perhaps a 'C'
Or an 'S'
Or maybe even a 'W'
So many letters you could've chosen when
You branded me
With your disapproval
With your control
With your self-righteousness
All because I refused, still refuse
To capitulate to your demands of
My rightful place in life as you saw it
My role in the world you desired
My submission to your will
You branded me
All because I dared, still dare
To stand tall and proud as a woman who
Embodies beauty, strength, and intelligence
Perhaps my lack of need
For your conformity frightened you

Well, fuck you, dear brander
I refuse to be
Branded
By you or anyone

Afterthought

I am no longer your
Afterthought
I once thought being your
Afterthought was enough
Anything to be in your life
When you offered me crumbs
I gobbled them up like I was starving
When you offered me driblets
I chugged them like I was dying of thirst
I accepted whatever you offered
I longed for you to see my worth
I wished for you to make me a priority
I wanted you to reach for me
I desired so much more than you offered
Then I realized the crumbs and driblets no longer filled me
Never really had
I looked at what you offered
It wasn't enough
Never really had been
So just know this
Take your crumbs and your driblets and go away
Or offer me the whole cake and champagne
Show me I am a priority to you
Reach out and pull me to you
It's not that hard to do
But you must
Give me everything I deserve
I can't accept anything less
I refuse to be anyone's
Afterthought
Not even yours

Box

You placed me
In a cute little white box
Adorned me with a red ribbon
Put me aside to open at your leisure
Thought I'd stay
Boxed in
Adorned
Exactly what you wanted
The perfection you imagined
A present for later
Something to anticipate
But you waited too long
Savoring the fantasy
Anticipating my need for you
Expecting my love
When you opened the box
You found
The nothing you created
When
You placed me
In a cute little white box
Adorned with a red ribbon

Me to Tell Me

"I needed me to tell me"
The words surprised me
When I heard them come from my mouth
The truth of them
Stopped me mid-step
Threw me off-balance
Left me speechless
For a second
I stood still in my thoughts
Realized I announced aloud
That I refuse to need permission
From anyone but me
For my likes
For my wants
For my needs
For my desires
For my loves
For my likes
For my life
In that moment I embraced
That I don't need nor do I want
External permission or approval
I really only need
Me to tell me

I Am Not

I am not
A woman you forget
I am not
A woman you hate
I am not
A woman you regret
I am not
A woman you anger
I am not
A woman you weaken
I am not
A woman you easily contain
I am not
A woman you easily win
I am not
A woman you wish to disappoint
I am not
A woman you want to hurt
I am not
A woman you betray
I am not
A woman you easily leave
Or so you said
Over and over and over
Yet
Somehow
You're no longer here

How to Seduce Me

It's harder than you might think
Or
Perhaps easier than you might think
To seduce me
Seduction is an art
Are you an artist?
Start with the prettiest of words
Not charming but sincere
Remind me of what I know about me
Not what you want me to be
Lift my virtues onto a pedestal
Exalting what I love about me
Love my imperfections
Noting how they highlight my perfections
That's a start
Keep going
Tease my thoughts
Tickle my interests
Caress my words
Play with my ideas
Kiss my secrets
Hug my fears
Embrace my desires
Revel in my strength
Support my weakness
Touch my vulnerability gently
Understand my beauty runs deeper than you see
Debate life's issues with me
Run your fingers through my arguments
Fill the voids in my heart with honesty
Heal the scars of yesterday with adoration

Respect my need to remain somewhat untouchable
Pull me closer when I run away
Show me your fear
Offer me your imperfection
Give me the best of you
Reach beyond the wall of words
I hide behind
See the gift of my pleasure
Once you know all of me
The naughty and the nice
Don't be scared
I'm not easily seduced
But I'm worth the effort

Universe in a Bowl

My universe in a bowl
You'd like that, wouldn't you?
Everything controlled, manageable, predictable
Try to put it there, I dare you
I'll burst that bowl from the inside
Watch it shatter into a million pieces
Freeing me
My universe expanding to its best self
Laughing at you
As you lament
Losing me
All because you tried to contain
My universe in a bowl
Silly, silly you

Never Lost

I am never lost
I may be adrift upon a sea
Of ever morphing waves
Tossing me toward my desires
Pulling me away from my loves
Drowning my dreams
Lifting me above my life
Forcing me to see
None of the things I wish to be
Everything I don't want to know
Taking me along for the ride
As I drift aimlessly far from shore
Wishing to beach my ever wandering mind
Hoping to land in welcoming arms
Celebrating that I cannot lose
What I most treasure
You may never see my worth
But it's of no consequence
Because life has taught me
No matter what you take from me
No matter how much or how little you value me
No matter how easily you walk away
Leaving me adrift on an ocean of change
I am never lost

I Am

I am love
I am hate
I am never
I am forever
I am truth
I am deception
I am trust
I am insecurity
I am courage
I am fear
I am strength
I am weakness
I am perfection
I am imperfection
I am life
I am death
I am all
I am nothing
I am simple
I am complex
I am what I am
I am what I am not
I am who I am
I am who I am not
I am
Me

Westbound Roots, Eastbound Roots

I stepped onto the train
The train bound eastward
To take me back to where
I began
To take me back to where
I walked away from you
In an effort to escape myself
I left a million ways
Before I ever said goodbye
Trapped by roots tangled around my legs
Tripping me with every step forward
I boarded a plane for a quick exit
Stretched those roots as far westward as I could
Stretched them to their limit
Stretched them until they thinned but refused to break
Embraced a brand new me
Pretended I could leave behind
My roots
My baggage
My love for you
Pretended I could be
A woman free of the experience that made me think
My love could never be good enough for you
The roots that tripped me
Refused to release their hold on me
Until I realized they still nourished me
And I reached out for the branches that once
Brought you to me
Wondering if our roots have been severed
As I turn my roots eastward again
Overlapping those I brought westward

But no longer tripping over the tangles
As I nurture the roots of yesterday
Moving forward into a stronger tomorrow

I No Longer Scare Me

I no longer scare me
Or do I?
I quashed me
To make life easier
To make you happy
To be what you wanted
Now I realize
What you complained about
What you found too abrasive
What you couldn't love
Was me
At the crux of all that you hated
Resides the heart of who I am
If I give up her
What do I have left to give?
If you hated so much about me
How was that ever love?
If I changed everything to make you love me
How come we don't work?
Maybe because no one can truly
Become someone else to please another
No matter the motivation
Not even for love
But is it love
When you ask someone to change who they are?
I allowed you to convince me
I needed fixed
Perhaps because I agreed on some level
Yet, it went too far
Now I'm lost
I've feared being me so long

Feared if I'm me no one will love me
Feared if I'm me I'll have no friends
Yet when I was me
I was surrounded by friends and family
People wanted to be near me
People wanted me to be happy
When I lost me and proclaimed myself happy
Immersed in your image of who I should be
Friends and family became lost to me
I feared allowing my truth to shine
I feared feeling anything
I feared thinking differently than you
I feared expressing my true self
Now I feel my emotions bursting forth
I'm unsure how to control them, contain them
My thoughts are taking on a life of their own
I can't keep them in line
I feel strength bubbling to the surface
Demanding I stand tall in my truth
I feel my needs bursting inside
Trying to find expression
I find my desires edging into my thoughts
Refusing to be denied
I feel pleasure invade my fantasies
Life can be so much more if we allow it
If I reach out for what I want
Will I get it
Will I find myself alone
Will I push everything good away
I need something that is real
I need joy in my connections
I need life in my existence
I need love that uplifts instead of stifles
I need released from the prison of fear

I've trapped myself in to avoid
The me I fear
At the crux of my existence
Is a woman who is fearless
I wish I could find her again
Then I could say a heartfelt
I no longer scare me

Right Time

I thought there'd be plenty of time
To be the woman I was meant to be
I lost track of me
Because I didn't understand
I couldn't wait to be me
I only had the moment
In front of me
Waiting for the right time
To be me
Cheated me out of the life
I could've lived
And left me with an empty shell
Designed to please
But hiding the substance within
Stole the strength I cherished
So I grab hold of time
Try to bend it to my will
To reclaim all those lost moments
When I waited for the right time
When I stood still
Supporting and nurturing your goals
Deceiving myself that
Your forward movement
Equaled my forward movement
Not realizing
Time wouldn't wait for me
While I waited for you
So now I grab hold of time
I'm done waiting
Life is mine to live
Time won't wait for me

And I can't wait for
The right time to embrace me
Not for even a minute more

Kind of Woman

I've never been the kind of woman who
Closes my eyes and leaps
Leans back and trusts someone to catch me
Expects others to reach out when I go quiet
Exposes my vulnerabilities easily
Reveals my heart without reservation

I've never been the kind of woman who
Runs from a fight
Gets intimidated from complications
Quits when life is difficult
Expects less than the best from myself
Accepts defeat

I've never been the kind of woman who
Begs for what I want
Demands perfection from others
Asks for more than I deserve
Expects others to sacrifice for me
Wants what I have no right to

I've never been the kind of woman who
Needs to be on a pedestal
Requires romantic gestures
Desires empty sentiments
Expects compliments
Revels in flattery

I've never been the kind of woman who
Needs someone else to fight my battles
Wants someone else to solve my problems

Allows other people to see me weak
Expects someone to fight for me
Relies on other people

I've never been the kind of woman who
Plays games with people's emotions
Manipulates people's thoughts
Ignores people's needs
Expects appreciation
Hurts people intentionally

I've never been the kind of woman who
Thinks I'm perfect
Gives up on being my best
Runs from a challenge
Expects forgiveness
Recognizes my strength

Or have I been
Exactly that kind of woman?
Perhaps I have simply hidden
The truth of who I am
From you
From me
From the world
Perhaps I just like to believe
I've never been the kind of woman who...

Used to Be

I used to be
The kind of girl
You didn't want to
Let down
Make angry
Disappoint
I used to be
The kind of girl
Who didn't tolerate
Game playing
Betrayal
Being ignored
I used to be
The kind of woman
Who commanded
Respect
Adoration
Loyalty
I used to be
The kind of woman
Who didn't tolerate
Disrespect
Indifference
Disloyalty
I used to be
The kind of woman
Who expected
Success
Cooperation
Growth
I used to be

The kind of woman
Who didn't accept
Defeat
Hindrance
Stagnation
I used to be
The kind of woman
Who valued
Strength
Integrity
Honesty
I used to be
The kind of woman
Who couldn't abide
Weakness
Duplicity
Dishonesty
I used to be
The kind of woman
I felt proud to be
Then I lost sight of
The kind of woman
I used to be
As I strived
To please
To be loveable
To be perfect
But perfection
Comes with a price
And that price
Was my truth
So now
I look at the woman
I used to be

And
I strive
To once again be
The woman
I used to be
When I look in the mirror
I once again see
The woman
I used to be
Staring back at me

New Improved Me

How can you not know me?
I split myself open
Showed you all my ugliness
Without mercy to either you or me
I wanted you to see me as perfect
Even as I drowned you in my imperfection
You accepted all that was wrong with me so easily
I found it easy to deny what was right with me
Soon I ceased to believe in my own sense of self
I handed my life over to you
I called it trust
I called it loyalty
I called it love
But really it was me denying my own existence
Denying even my right to an existence
I became a shadow in my own life
I became a reflection of expectations
I lost all sense of self
One day I stepped back into my life
Stepped out of the shadows
Shattered the mirror of expectations
Found my sense of self
Embraced life again
Understood
Love, loyalty, trust
Aren't about sacrificing one's self
When I honored myself
Perfection and imperfection
I became whole again
I discovered the key to
Love, loyalty, trust

Lies first in
Loving myself
Honoring myself
Trusting myself
Empowering myself
So I stood strong and waited
Not daring to blink
To see if you'd love
The new, improved me

Reclamation

I dug deep
Tried to reclaim
The girl I once was
She was stronger than
The woman I'd become

I uncovered
The girl I was
Before...
It was so long ago
But I miss that girl
Miss her so very much
She fought hard to survive
After...

But the woman I became
Slowly buried her under
Accusation, denial, pain
If she no longer existed
Perhaps what happened
Would cease to have happened

As the woman in the mirror
Denied the spark of the girl
By not looking into her eyes
I discovered life was easier
If I gave up my power
Easier but not really living

As I kissed the girl within
Revealed the treasure of her

I discovered something shocking
Something that at first saddened me
She refused to be reclaimed
What had happened happened
Even she, dormant as she lay, changed
I finally cried tears for her
I grieved the girl lost to
Betrayal
Who considered herself
Damaged, weakened, undeserving

When my tears finally dried
I discovered she didn't need reclaimed
She'd lived in me all along
Screaming to be released from
The grave I buried her in
Raring to be incorporated
Into the woman I'd become

In that moment
The strong girl
Buried deep inside
This weak woman
Emerged in a merger
Creating
Not a reclaimed girl
But a stronger woman
Made resilient by experience

The Sum of My Parts

I am more than
The sum of my parts
You might see my smile
You might stare at my cleavage
You might notice the curve of my waist
You might admire my ass
You might let your gaze linger on my tight calves
You might long to touch the softness of my inner thighs
You might imagine the kiss of my lips
You might dream about my tongue's ability to please
You might fantasize about the heaven between my legs
You might look at me
And only see
The sum of my parts
You might desire to devour me
You might want to dominate me
You might even wish to pleasure me
But
If you can't see the beauty of my soul
If you can't see the brilliance of my mind
If you can't see the generosity of my heart
If you can't see my thoughts as equal to yours
If you can't see my emotions as important
If you can't see I'm as much a person as you
If you can't appreciate me for whom I am
Once you get past
The sum of my parts
If you can't understand
Why knowing me
Is a privilege
If you can't see

I am so much more than
The sum of my parts
If you can't embrace
All I offer
You don't deserve
To enjoy
The sum of my parts
I decide
Whether you treat me with
The respect, appreciation, and consideration
I deserve
If you don't
You'll be left to fantasize about
The sum of my parts
And
You'll never have the honor
Of knowing me
Mind, heart, soul, and body
And knowing me is an honor
I promise you
I'm worth so much more than
The sum of my parts
Do you think you deserve
To know all of me?
Then prove it

Restraint

I stare into the future
Wonder
Should I adopt
Restraint
Constraint
Abandon
I've embraced restraint
Until I felt shackled
I've adopted constraint
Until I felt imprisoned
I've welcomed abandon
Until I felt wild
I'm learning to balance
Restraint
Constraint
Abandon
Or am I...

Sometimes I long
To cut my restraints
To escape constraint
To hide from abandon
The conundrum of
When to practice
Restraint
Constraint
Abandon
Leaves me motionless
In a sea of indecision

So tomorrow

I'll follow my instincts
And hope they reveal
When to practice restraint
And when to cut the shackles
When to practice constraint
And when to escape imprisonment
When to practice abandon
And when to rein in my wildness
Because listening to others' expectations
Sure as hell hasn't freed me to balance
Restraint
Constraint
Abandon
In any way that approaches fulfillment
And allows my truth to shine

When I'm free to choose
When
Restraint
Constraint
Abandon
Work best for me
No matter what
Anyone else says
I'm free to share me
With me
With you
With the world
In the fullness of my being
Without extremes
Encumbering my truth

Button

You pushed that button
You know the one
The one that gets me going
The one that changes everything
The one that breaks me
Perhaps you regret it now
But you knew what you were doing
Don't try to deny it
When you pushed it
You smiled
Perhaps you thought I'd wilt into your whims
I stood on my own
I refused to take your bait
I broke rather than bend to your will
Even though I broke I wasn't broken
I found my own nourishment
Repaired the break in my structure
Rebuilt my strength
Recovered my life
Stood taller than ever
Walked away from your attempts to break me
Bet now you curse the day you decided to
Push that particular button

Contradictory Me

Today
I am beautiful
I am ugly
I am strong
I am weak
I am wonderful
I am terrible
I am loving
I am hateful
I am generous
I am greedy
I am loveable
I am despicable
I am talented
I am untalented
I am intelligent
I am stupid
I am resilient
I am unadaptable
I am tenacious
I am hesitant
I am rational
I am irrational
I am nice
I am naughty
I am sweet
I am cruel
I am perfect
I am imperfect
I am everything
I am nothing

I am revealed
I am hidden
Today
I am just me

According to Me

I worried what you thought
I worried what he thought
I worried what she thought
I worried what the world thought
Then one day I looked in the mirror
I thought about what I wanted
My nieces
To feel about themselves
To see in themselves
To hear in their heads
To believe about themselves
To understand about life
To know about being women
A sudden realization hit me
My message to them applied to me
So I spoke the words to my reflection
I am worthy of love
I am worthy of respect
I am worthy of honor
I am worthy of loyalty
I am worthwhile
I love who I am
Sacrificing me is never an option
I have the right pursue *my* dreams
I am responsible for my life
No one gets to steal my strength
No one gets to control my happiness
No one gets to crush my spirit
No one gets to subjugate me
I am enough as I am
I am loveable

I am beautiful
I am special
I am the perfect me, flaws and virtues
I don't need fixed
I have the power to learn from my mistakes
My missteps alone don't define me
I must risk failure to succeed
I deserve to be treated lovingly
I deserve happiness
I deserve only the best
I must never allow another to define me
Accepting support isn't a sign of weakness
Being tough isn't the same as being strong
Strength doesn't always look strong
I have to remember when I look outside me
It doesn't matter what you think
It doesn't matter what he thinks
It doesn't matter what she thinks
It doesn't matter what the world thinks
The only thing
That matters is
Who I am
According to me

Judgment

I stood before you
Silent
Uttered not a word
Made not a sound
Slowly removed
One layer
Then another
Then another
My eyes fixed on yours
Watching to see your reaction
Revealing
First a hint of what was beneath
Then a little more
Hesitating as I reached the more vulnerable layers
You encouraged me
To show you
Each layer in turn
Urged me to expose more
Until I stood before you
Bare, vulnerable, naked
Awaiting your judgment
Unable to read your expression
I waited and watched you
As you stared at my nudity
Standing before you
My layers puddled
At my feet
Surrounding me in a sea
A sea churning with exposure
Leaving me open, vulnerable
And still I stood

Ready to walk away
My chin trembled
I blinked back a tear
I'd never felt so alive
As I stared into your eyes
Awaiting your judgment
Knowing I'd already passed mine
And I was the victor
No matter your reaction
Because I was strong enough
To stand before you
Bare, vulnerable, naked
And know your judgment
Really only defined
What happened between us
Not who I am

Tomorrow

When I cry for tomorrow
And tomorrow doesn't come
Because yesterday blocks her path
I'm forced to stand in today
To find the strength and beauty
Inherent in the moment I inhabit
Somehow when I'm forced to
Stand in today
The tears for tomorrow dry
Yesterday dissolves into a salty puddle
When I embrace the strength and beauty
Inherent in the moment I inhabit
I discover that strength and beauty
Emanates from inside me
Yesterday becomes a rocky, wet path of discovery
Today shows me how far I've traveled
Tomorrow stands before me untraveled and welcoming
And I smile for tomorrow

Rebirth

I asked myself
Once
Many years ago
Who would care if I died?
Who would even notice?
I didn't ask to belittle myself
I didn't ask out of self-pity
I didn't ask to find drama
But to assess my life
Had I made a difference?
Had I done anything that mattered?
Had I reached for my potential?
As I sat alone in front of the fire
And focused on those questions
The answers became clear
I fought them
The truth was
Few would notice
Even fewer would care
I turned inward
Focused on why
Discovered answers
I didn't like
I was so self-absorbed
All I cared about was my own pain
I had ceased to see joy in life
I had ceased to offer anything positive
I had worked to disappear
I had denied myself
My dreams, my goals, my desires
I had denied my existence

Even to me
I closed my eyes
Tried to hold back a tear or ten
They rebelled
Even my tears refused to listen to me
When my eyes were dry
My heart again felt full
My mind again felt engaged
My soul again felt receptive
My purpose again felt energized
I remembered I once had much to offer
Friends
Family
The world
I reached out for the girl I once was
To discover the woman I was meant to be
And stepped into my future

To My Teenage Self

If I could have a moment of your time
My Teenage Self
I'd tell you
You are beautiful
You are loveable
You can have both love and success
You are worth the world
You are not alone
Being different is okay, desirable even

I'd tell you
Have more fun
Don't take life so seriously
You have the right to laugh
To laugh out loud and often
You have the right to play
To play hard and often
You have the right to love
To love hard and risk pain
You have the right to be loved
To be loved deeply and passionately

I'd tell you
To slow down
Life happens in its own time
You can't force it
So enjoy it
Don't wait for the future
To be happy
To have fun
To love

To live
To enjoy life
Live in this moment, every moment

I'd tell you
Do what you enjoy
You don't have to be perfect to have fun
You don't even have to be good at it
Golf
Bowl
Shoot pool
Learn new things
Attempt things that interest you
Don't be ashamed to try
Just go for it
Laugh and play to your heart's content
Enjoy yourself
You only get one life
Go for it without caring what other people say

I'd tell you
To keep dancing even if you're the only one on the floor
To stand up for what you believe
To listen to others but keep your sense of self
To never allow your voice to be weakened by anyone
To never suppress who you are to please another
To embrace those who love you
To walk away from those who mistreat you
To never believe you have to earn love
Love not freely given is never love only obligation
Obligation is never enough
Allow yourself to feel vulnerable but never be gullible

I'd tell you

The person who makes fun of you
Won't matter in a few years
The person who ignores you
Will someday pursue your friendship
The person who laughs at you
For writing will someday love your work
The person who rejects you
Will regret it someday
The person you call best friend
May desert you but you'll survive
The person you trust most may betray you
But you'll find your own truth
When people come and go in your life
It's not a reflection on your worth

I'd tell you
Listen to your instincts
Listen to your heart
Listen to your thoughts
Don't let others change who you are
You may fail, you may get hurt
But you'll always get back up and you'll thrive

I'd tell you
Someday you'll look back
See
You were always stronger
Than you thought
You were always more intelligent
Than you gave yourself credit for
You were always more beautiful
Than you believed
You were always more compassionate
Than you knew

You were always capable of love
You were always capable of achieving your dreams
You always had everything you needed to be the very best you

I'd tell you
The labels you're assigned will cease to matter someday
You'll be stronger and more compassionate
You'll figure out that happiness comes from within
You'll understand that you have choices
You'll find a way to live from a place of love
You'll learn to accept that it's okay if not everyone likes you
You'll figure out forgiveness releases you, not the other person
You'll even learn how to forgive without forgetting the lesson
Life doesn't begin and end with where you reside today

I'd tell you
You'll travel the world
You'll meet people who understand you
You'll meet people who love you
You'll meet people who want to be near you
You'll meet people who astound you
You'll meet people who accept you
Without trying to change anything about you
But who support you as you grow into your best self
You'll be surrounded by incredible people and experiences

I'd tell you
You don't need to be perfect
You don't need to be everything others expect you to be
You don't have to take care of everyone
You don't have to save the whole world
You have the right and responsibility to do what's best for you
Your job is first and foremost to be you

I'd tell you
My Teenage Self
You are enough

Courage

Strength
I've always found
Even in my weakest moments
Courage
I've always thought I had
Even when I've been most scared
I'm not so sure anymore
I look back at the moments
I considered courageous
I suddenly realize
There was no courage
Only bravado
I never showed you me
I never gave you me
I arranged my life
To protect my vulnerabilities
Rather than face them
I chose the option
Less likely to lead to true intimacy
Rather than risk rejection
Rather than risk a broken heart
Rather than risk losing you
Of course walking away
Was losing you, too
Now I search for the courage
I wish I'd had then
Because once again
I lack the courage
To speak the truth in my heart
To show you how I feel
To risk your rejection of me

To risk you breaking my heart
To risk losing your friendship, too
But if I'm silent
I'll lose you anyway
Just like before
My heart has no doubt
So I search for the courage
Because if I take the risk
I just may discover
You want the same thing I do
You can offer me the intimacy I desire
You might just offer me the love I deserve
You and I can be good together
We can build something excellent together
Without the courage
To speak up
To risk my heart
Now I have to question
The truth of my
Strength
Without strength
Can courage exist?

World of the Woman

Bold and beautiful
Shy and sweet
Lovely and light
Strong and sexy
Testing and tantalizing
Feisty and feminine
Reaching for reality
Feeding into fantasy
Obsessing over obedience
Rebelling against rules
Striving for stillness
Healing hurts
Delivering dreams
Sacrificing to succeed
Grasping life's goals
Understanding what's hidden underneath
Contradictions creating commonality
World of the woman

You Might

You might break my bones
You might bruise my skin
You might tear my muscles
You might hold me down
You might pen me in
You might criticize me
You might belittle me
But
My spirit you may not touch
My soul you may not injure
My self you may not capture
My strength you may not weaken
My glow you may not dull
My beauty you may not mar
Because
No matter what
I am me
That you cannot change
That you cannot damage
That you cannot destroy
Who I am survives and thrives
And always will

Moment in Your Memory

I am merely a moment in your memory
A commentary on empty romance
Leaving a lemony taste in your mouth
Clammy hands embracing molten passion
Though I'll never be your porn star
My teeny net captured your fantasy
You saw me as a lone poem
Complete with juicy melon juice dripping
With the creamy nectar of a cayenne hot trance
Until that day I became your enemy
With the omen that the memento of my love
Would never leave your temple
I became a mopey polymer tycoon
Holding a metronome in your thoughts
As I stood with the strength of a myrtle
Racy to the end with my cyan aura
Never content to be anyone's crony or peon
But only to embrace my coy inner anemone
Someday you will see my strength was never manly
It simply grew out of the royal mercy
I commonly offer because
I am one on which to rely
Until my plenty becomes empty
Leaving me poor and teary
Awaiting the moon's mantle
To ante up my aptly divined tome
So I can play my ace
And cover my heart in calmer lace
As you lament your loss and I meanly parlay
I'm not any port to be ignored
I'm not prey to be captured

I'm not a pony to be ridden
I'm not a peony to be picked
I'm not a room to be cleaned
I'm not a menace to cremate
I'm not a point to be made moot
I deserve no penalty for my crayon employment
I'll forever play my off-tempo beat
Hoping against hope you'll someday see
I'm more than a moment in your memory

Weed

Biting cold
Nipping at exposed skin
Sun playing trickster
Bright but not warm
Skies blue between
Fields of clouds overhead
Plants budding
In spring pastels
Lots of yellow
Still my eye is drawn to
Weeds
Weeds everywhere
I remember as a child
Picking dandelions for bouquets
Dandelions are a lovely yellow
Until one day someone told me
Dandelions are weeds
In an instant it went from pretty to ugly
Without changing a single thing about itself
In our search for perfection
In our desire for symmetry
In our quest for uniformity
We forget
A weed is just a plant in an unwanted place
It isn't bad or good
It just lives where it's not wanted
We see it as undesirable because it mars
Uniformity
We refuse to see the beauty in imperfection
We resist the idea of nature's beauty
Whether in our bodies or our communities

We sculpt and mold and morph
Our landscapes, our worlds, our selves
To please people we don't even know, let alone like
In hopes they'll see our value
As I walked I pondered
Whether it's better to be a weed
Wild and free
Growing wherever I sprout
Or a sculpted, maintained plant
Growing where someone else wants me
I've grown tired of being told
Where, when, and how to grow
I've decided to embrace
My inner
Weed

Flames of My Life

Staring into the flames
Gratitude on my mind
Flames reach higher
As gratitude fills my heart
With each negative thought
The flames die back
As if my negativity
Can douse the flame
When positive thoughts return
The flames reach higher again
The flames dance
Red and yellow
Against dark logs
Embers fall from the wood
My negativity burning up
In those flames
Positive energy fills my body
Creativity finds a new source
Gratitude inhabits my soul
Gratitude and negativity
Dancing a rhythm in flames
Scorching one another
Fighting to survive
In my heart
Fighting for dominance
In my thoughts
Fighting to guide
My life
The dance of
Gratitude and negativity
In the flames of my life

Strength in Silhouette

Standing in the sun
Silhouetted against life
Waiting, watching, wondering
What will next challenge
The strength held within
Looking toward the sun
Back to the night
Flexing muscles
Preparing for the fight
Knowing that my strength
May fluctuate
May hide
May feel weakened
But when the moon rises
The stars will highlight
The silhouette of strength
Hidden within the recesses
Awaiting release
To be more than a shadow
Wishing to be more than
Strength in Silhouette

PRAISE FOR T. L. COOPER'S BOOKS

Memory in Silhouette

"…pithy examination of relational memories should help every poet discover an inner part of their own memories. I highly recommend this poetic study in life lived and memories examined." – Auburn McCanta, author of All the Dancing Birds

Reflections in Silhouette:

"…Brave enough to lower the curtain into her own heart, T.L. gives the reader that certain leverage where one might be able to find the strength, upon reflection, to go forward into the bright sunshine of their own new day…" - Ray Ellis, author of the Nate Richards Series.

Love in Silhouette:

"…Love in Silhouette" is a delightfully honest and open-faced collection of poetry that leaves you feeling as though you have peeked in on intimate moments of the author's love life…" - Mary Braun, co-author of Opposites Attract: A Haiku Tete-a-Tete.

"…Cooper's poems are lyrical. Don't be fooled into thinking that this is simply a collection of silly love poems. They pull you in to explore the depths of love and all that goes with it…" - Lauren Carr, author of the Mac Faraday Series.

All She Ever Wanted:

"…A thoughtful, insightful look into the changing human mind and spirit evoked by an interracial friendship, All She Ever Wanted is a superbly written, highly recommended novel showcasing a theme that is as historic and universal as interracial human experience, and contemporary as today's newspaper headlines…" - Midwest Book Review.

ABOUT THE AUTHOR

T. L. Cooper is an author and poet whose poetry has been described as making poetry accessible to people who usually don't read poetry. Her poems, short stories, articles, and essays have appeared online, in books, and in magazines. Her published books include a novel, *All She Ever Wanted*, and her Silhouette Poetry Series. She grew up on a farm in Tollesboro, Kentucky. She studied corrections and psychology at Eastern Kentucky University. When not writing, she enjoys yoga, golf, and traveling. Learn more at www.tlcooper.com.

Made in the USA
Las Vegas, NV
14 May 2021